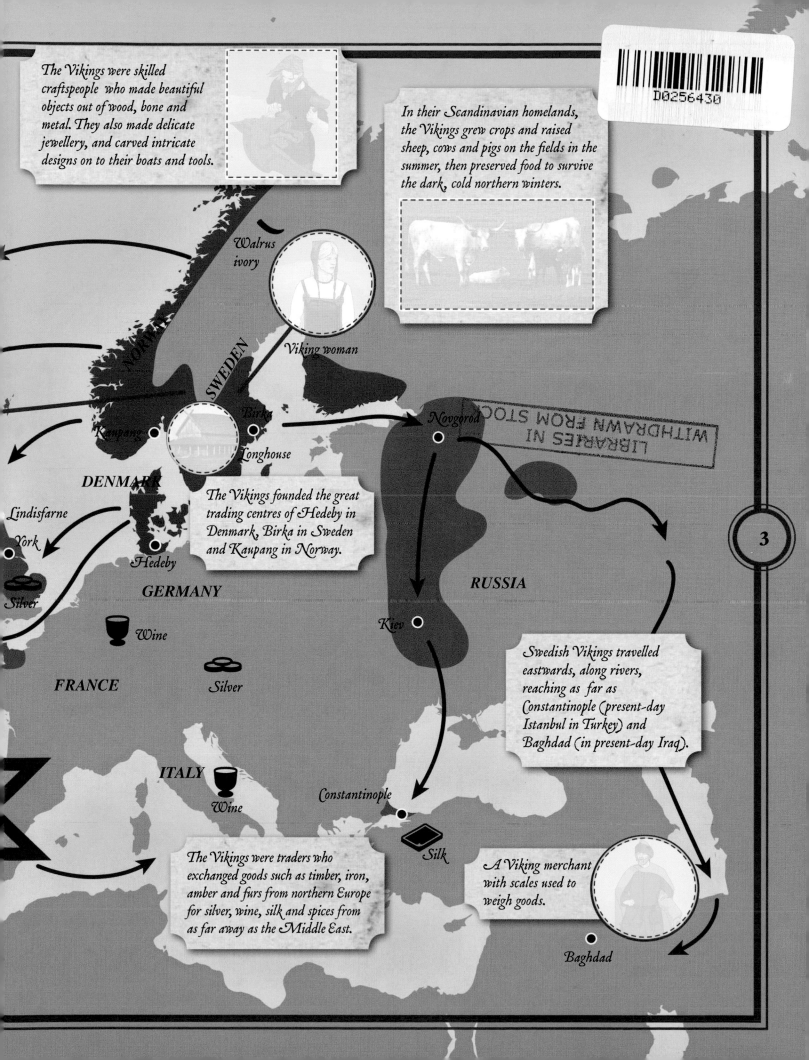

The Vikings were skilled craftspeople who made beautiful objects out of wood, bone and metal. They also made delicate jewellery, and carved intricate designs on to their boats and tools.

In their Scandinavian homelands, the Vikings grew crops and raised sheep, cows and pigs on the fields in the summer, then preserved food to survive the dark, cold northern winters.

Walrus ivory

Viking woman

NORWAY

SWEDEN

Birka

Kaupang

Longhouse

DENMARK

The Vikings founded the great trading centres of Hedeby in Denmark, Birka in Sweden and Kaupang in Norway.

Lindisfarne

York

Silver

Hedeby

GERMANY

Wine

FRANCE

Silver

Novgorod

RUSSIA

Kiev

Swedish Vikings travelled eastwards, along rivers, reaching as far as Constantinople (present-day Istanbul in Turkey) and Baghdad (in present-day Iraq).

ITALY

Wine

Constantinople

Silk

The Vikings were traders who exchanged goods such as timber, iron, amber and furs from northern Europe for silver, wine, silk and spices from as far away as the Middle East.

A Viking merchant with scales used to weigh goods.

Baghdad

3

A VIKING LONGSHIP

Longships or dragon-ships (drakkar) were fast-moving ships designed to transport Viking warriors. With their dragon-shaped prows and battle-hardened crew, they were a sight to strike fear into peoples' hearts as they approached foreign shores.

The carved dragon head on the prow (front) of the ship was made to frighten enemies and was believed to scare away evil spirits at sea.

The square sail was made up of strips of wool or linen, waterproofed with animal fat. The sail and mast could be raised and lowered quickly to take advantage of the winds.

The sailors had nowhere to hide from high waves. On long voyages, the crew would steer the ship to a shore where they could camp overnight.

The iron anchor was used to hold the prow of the ship on the shore, rather than to keep the ship in position in deep water.

The hull of a Viking longship was made up of overlapping curved oak planks, called strakes, joined by iron rivets. The gaps between the strakes were filled with wool dipped in tar to stop sea water leaking in.

At up to 36 metres in length, these ships could carry 60 warriors, who took turns at the oars. The oars fitted through holes along the top plank of the ship's hull.

Parts of the ship were decorated with beautiful carvings.

A heavy oar was attached to the stern (rear) of the ship as a rudder.

The design of the ship was shallow, allowing the craft to land on a beach, where the warriors could leap out and attack at once, and then sail away quickly.

Warriors' shields rested on shield battens along the topmost strake on the ship as the crew prepared to enter a battle.

A VIKING WARRIOR

For a Viking warrior there was nothing more glorious than dying in battle. Toughened by life in rugged northern countries and perilous sea voyages, the warriors of Scandinavia soon gained a deadly reputation.

Iron helmets with eye, nose and sometimes neck guards were worn by chieftains. Most Viking warriors couldn't afford helmets and wore leather caps.

As well as a sword, Viking warriors might carry a spear, an axe or a dagger.

Viking warriors did not wear uniforms. They wore their own knee-length chain-mail armour or sleeveless, padded leather jerkins (jackets).

The Vikings' double-edged swords were used with a single hand. They were sometimes given names, such as "Battleflame" or "Mail-Biter".

Woollen cloaks were fastened with a brooch on the right shoulder, to help leave the sword arm free.

A tough wooden shield was raised to fend off enemy sword thrusts or arrow attacks. At its centre was an iron boss, which protected the hand.

Ankle boots were made of tanned animal skin. Vikings may have also worn woollen socks to keep warm.

VIKING ATTACKERS

The Vikings made lightning fast raids on islands such as Britain and Ireland in search of riches. The people in the coastal towns were largely unprepared for them. The most frightening of the Viking warriors were the "berserkers".

This Viking chess piece shows a berserker. He has a mad stare, a raised sword, and chews on his shield like a wild animal.

Before battle, these men would work themselves into a furious rage, sometimes even frothing at the mouth!

The word "berserk" comes from the Norse word "bear-sark", meaning "bear shirt". Berserkers wore fur skins and acted like ferocious bears to scare their opponents.

Viking boys were trained to fight from a young age, using wooden swords and shields to practise with. They may have joined raids from the age of 16.

A VIKING NOBLEWOMAN

Viking women ran the homes and farms and raised the children, while the men hunted, fished, traded and went to battle. Women wore long, loose dresses fastened with brooches and sometimes decorated with fine embroidery.

Necklaces were made of glass (left) or amber beads. Amber, from Denmark, was traded with precious metals, with which the Vikings could make fine jewellery.

Combs were made from bone or sometimes deer antlers and decorated with fine designs.

Nobles wore jewellery to display their wealth. Neck bands, arm bands and rings were crafted in silver and gold.

This woman's woollen overdress is held up by brooches. Each brooch bears an ornate design. She would sometimes wear a shawl over her shoulders.

This wealthy woman is wearing an underdress made of linen, and an outerdress made of wool. Clothes were sometimes coloured with natural dyes, such as a brown pigment made from walnuts.

Viking women were skilled at spinning and weaving, using a loom to make cloth out of wool. Rich women wore expensive silks from abroad. Golden embroidery and fur trimmings also adorned the clothes of nobles.

Shoes were made from calf or goat skin, with laces tied around the ankle.

VIKING PIONEERS

As the Viking population in Scandinavia increased, farm land became scarcer. So brave Viking explorers headed west to seek out new lands where they could build settlements and farms.

In AD 982, Erik the Red set sail for Greenland. This big island was very bleak, but he named it Greenland to entice other Vikings to join him. The Vikings raised livestock and hunted whales on Greenland for about 400 years. Erik's main settlement was at Brattahlid.

In AD 874, Ingólfur Arnarson sailed westwards from Norway to Iceland. He brought timber to build shelters, and settled in the bay that is now Iceland's capital Reykjavik. By AD 930, up to 20,000 Vikings had settled on Iceland, raising sheep and making tools with the local iron.

ICELAND

GREENLAND

Brattahlid

Reykjavik

NORWAY

SWEDEN

SCOTLAND

DENMARK

NORTH AMERICA

ATLANTIC OCEAN

IRELAND

ENGLAND

GERMANY

L'Anse aux Meadows

NEWFOUNDLAND

N

W E

S

KEY

Viking homelands

Viking settlements

Viking routes

FRANCE

SPAIN

Leif "the Lucky" Erikson was the son of Eric the Red. Around AD 1000 he travelled thousands of kilometres to an island now called Newfoundland, Canada. He called it "Vinland", possibly mistaking the native huckleberries for grape vines. The Vikings settled here for a while but they were often attacked by local tribes.

"Knarr" is the Norse word for a type of ship built for long sea voyages. Their hulls were wider and deeper than those of a longship. They were used to carry cargo such as timber, livestock and weapons as well as food and drink.

VIKING RAID!

The Vikings knew that monasteries were full of treasures, and that they were poorly defended by monks. One of their first assaults, in AD 793, was on the island of Lindisfarne off the north-east coast of England. Their bloodthirsty attack on its monastery shook England to the core.

There had been a monastery on the small island of Lindisfarne for 158 years before the Vikings arrived. The famous monk Saint Cuthbert was buried here and his shrine became a place of pilgrimage. The island was known as Holy Island.

About 30 monks plus helpers worked and prayed at Lindisfarne at the time of the raid. The monks were unarmed. Many were slaughtered on the beach. The rest were taken away to be sold as slaves.

The Vikings not only attacked and killed the people on the island, but also their cattle and sheep, which they stole for food.

Treasures in the monastery may have included crosses made of precious metals, leather-bound and decorated books, donations made by pilgrims and chalices similar to this one.

The low beaches on Lindisfarne were perfect for a Viking longship landing. The ship could unload its crew of warriors right onto the sand, then be pushed out and rowed away, just as quickly, once the raid was over.

One treasure that the Viking raid failed to capture was the Lindisfarne Gospels. This beautifully painted collection of Bible stories was worked on by the monk Eadfrith.

This 9th-century gravestone depicts the Viking raid on Lindisfarne. A small army of Vikings attack with raised swords and axes.

FOOD AND DRINK

The Vikings' daily diet consisted of simple foods such as bread, cheese, grains and fruit. On special feast nights they would dine on roast meat, such as pork or lamb.

At the centre of a Viking home was the hearth, an open fire. Over this hung an iron cauldron where food was prepared.

The Vikings grew cabbages, beans and peas, as well as cereals, such as oats, barley (below) and rye. Seaweed was also a healthy source of vitamins.

Vikings ate two meals a day – in the early morning and in the early evening. They didn't use forks, just a knife and fingers.

Vikings drank beer and mead, a brew made from honey.

Bread was made using barley flour and baked over a griddle on the fire. Without yeast, Viking bread did not rise.

Vikings kept cattle, sheep, pigs, goats and chickens. They also hunted animals and fished. Dinner might include sausage spiced with thyme, stewed seagull, wild boar, herring, eggs, cheese and porridge.

To survive the cold winters, Vikings preserved and stored their food. Fish was hung up to dry in the wind or pickled in sea salt.

VIKING SOCIETY

Viking society was divided into three groups. At the top were the king and the jarls, or nobles. Below were the freemen, including warriors, craftspeople, merchants and farmers. And at the bottom of society were the thralls, or slaves.

Jarls and land-owning men met once a year to solve disputes and agree on laws at an outdoor assembly known as a "Thing".

The king had his own private army and could order any freemen to join him in battle. He had vast treasures taken from foreign raids and lived in the grandest of houses.

The jarl, or earl, was the local chieftain. He had a duty to raise a fighting force for the king but he could also demand taxes from the people who lived on his land.

Most Vikings were freemen, or karls. They were usually farmers, hunters, traders or craftsmen. Freemen could be called upon to fight for their jarl or king.

Thralls, or slaves, were often prisoners, captured during Viking raids. A thrall would be expected to work in their owner's house, or as a farmhand.

A VIKING LONGHOUSE

Most Viking homes were simple wooden or stone buildings, usually one storey high and consisting of one main room. Families would live and work in the same building, and sometimes shared their space with their animals.

Beds were positioned around the hearth for warmth. Pillows and mattresses were made with feathers, blankets were made of wool, and furs were used for extra warmth.

Scandinavian winters were cold, so many animals were brought indoors. Though the house could get smelly, the extra bodies helped keep it warm.

Light in the dark houses was provided by lamps. These were iron or stone bowls filled with animal fat or fish oil, and lit using a wick, like a candle.

Girls were taught how to spin and weave. First they would spin the wool to make yarn. Then, a large wooden loom was used to weave the yarn into cloth for blankets, clothing, ship sails or tapestries.

The roof was made of thatch or turf. With no windows, smoke from the fire escaped through the door and a small hole in the roof. The house could get rather smoky.

Wealthier families hung up tapestries. These added colour, and kept out draughts.

Walls were made from wood or wattle — long woven branches covered in dried mud. There were few or no windows and no carpets. Floors were just trodden earth.

Food was kept in pots and wooden barrels, while clothes and valuables were stored in chests.

The toilet was just a hidden hole in the ground, outside. Despite the filthy look of many homes, Vikings themselves were fairly clean, taking regular baths.

ARTS AND CRAFTS

The Vikings were talented craftspeople who made remarkable weapons, jewellery, clothes and tapestries, some with elaborate designs.

Viking carpenters were skilled at building tough and fast-moving ships from wood. Some had dragon figureheads with intricate, entwined patterns, such as this one discovered at Oseberg, Norway (left). The carvings were also often painted.

Sometimes Viking axe heads were inlaid with beautiful silver patterns (right). Metalworkers also crafted fine jewellery for both men and women. Ornate brooches were used as pins to fasten clothes, while arm and neck rings, were a display of wealth.

Necklaces were made from amber, patterned glass beads (right) or precious stones. Some carried pendants. The image of a hammer belonging to the thunder god Thor was often worn as a pendant (left). The Vikings thought the pendant would protect them from storms at sea.

Owning gold and silver was a sign of wealth. This mount for a horse's bridle (left) is made of bronze covered in gold leaf.

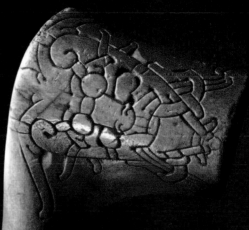

Walrus tusks, animal bones and antlers were used to make delicate dress pins, combs and walking-stick handles (above).

A fragment of a 12th-13th century Viking tapestry from Baldishol, Norway, shows that the Vikings produced colourful fabrics. This tapestry, dating from the end of the Viking age, features warriors on horses.

VIKING SAGAS

The Vikings loved to share stories of adventure called sagas. Their sagas tell of kings, powerful dragon slayers and epic battles between gods and giants.

Sagas were not written down but memorised and spoken out aloud. Around the 13th century, they were eventually written down, which is why we know about them today.

Viking kings appointed a poet, or skald. He entertained guests with tales of the king's brave deeds. These tales were passed down through generations of storytellers.

In one saga the Viking god Thor boasts of his greatness to the giants. They challenge him to lift their cat, but he cannot move even one of its paws. Thor discovers that the cat is the gods' huge serpent in disguise. Thor vows to take revenge for being tricked.

Snorri Sturluson was a 13th-century Icelandic poet. He wrote a handbook on poetry and also a history of the kings of Norway.

THE SAGA OF SIGURD

Sigurd is the hero of one of the most famous Norse sagas, "Volsunga Saga". According to this saga, Sigurd kills the great dragon Fafnir and eats his heart, thus gaining a very special knowledge.

SIGURD FIGHTS THE DRAGON FAFNIR

1.

The dragon Fafnir's brother, Regin the blacksmith, urges the brave Sigurd to reclaim a hoard of gold once owned by the great god Odin. The fiery Fafnir guards the hoard.

2.

Sigurd hides in a pit waiting for Fafnir. When the dragon passes above, Sigurd stabs him and bathes in his blood. The blood makes Sigurd invincible.

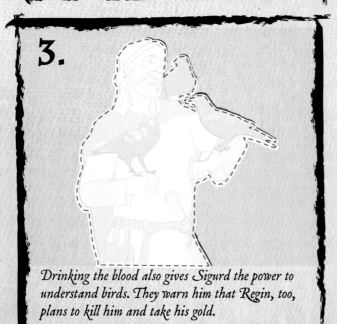

3.

Drinking the blood also gives Sigurd the power to understand birds. They warn him that Regin, too, plans to kill him and take his gold.

4.

Sigurd kills Regin and regains the gold. He roasts Fafnir's heart and eats it, thus gaining the power to see into the future.

RUNES AND RUNESTONES

The Vikings used an alphabet made up of runes, which were easy to scratch onto wood or stone because they had straight lines. Runes were carved on memorial stones to fallen warriors or family members.

The Viking alphabet was called the "futhark", after its first six letters. There were 16 runes in the futhark.

f u th a r k h n

i a s t b m l R

Runestones were often colourfully painted. This copy of a 10th-century runestone from Jelling, Denmark, has an image of Christ on one side and a memorial to the parents of King Harald Bluetooth on the other.

The runes on this stone from Gripsholm, Sweden, are written in the shape of a snake. The stone was carved in memory of a Viking named Harald, who died on a voyage to the East.

This bone found in Lund, Sweden, is carved with the 16 runes of the futhark.

DANEGELD

The rulers of England were desperate to stop the Viking invasions of their shores. They even paid the Vikings large sums of money to stop the raids.

In AD 991 a fleet of 93 Viking ships led by Olaf Tryggvason landed on the southeast coast of England. The English forces struggled to keep them at bay. King Aethelred the Unready (right) paid them huge sums of silver to persuade them to go. But the price of paying the Vikings to stop the raids just went up and up.

It is thought that in AD 1002, on the feast day of St Brice, Aethelred tried a new tack to deter the Viking raids. He ordered the killing of many Viking settlers in England. But the killings had little effect and England was invaded by Sweyn Forkbeard, King of Denmark (below).

In southeast England, a similar bargain was struck between Viking raiders and the people of Kent. This money was called Danegeld, meaning "Danish tribute". It rarely worked. Once paid, the Vikings returned for more money.

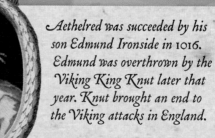

Aethelred was succeeded by his son Edmund Ironside in 1016. Edmund was overthrown by the Viking King Knut later that year. Knut brought an end to the Viking attacks in England.

21

CLASH IN CONSTANTINOPLE

During the 9th and 10th centuries the Vikings made surprise attacks on the magnificent city of Constantinople (modern-day Istanbul, Turkey). The attack in AD 907 was their most successful.

The attack was launched by Prince Oleg "the Wise" of Novgorod (a city now in modern-day Russia). In AD 907 he set sail with 2,000 longships and 80,000 men to capture Constantinople.

Constantinople was the capital of the Byzantine Empire. It had grand palaces decorated with mosaics, huge statues and imposing arches.

The Vikings who Oleg took to invade Constantinople were from the city of Kiev and were known as the "Rus". The word means "rowers", and may be the origin of the name for Russia.

At the heart of the city was the magnificent church of Hagia Sophia (left), which still looks over Istanbul today.

The markets of Constantinople were legendary. They sold exotic wares such as silk and spices from China, and silver from Afghanistan. The Vikings had visited them before to trade in furs, honey, weapons and slaves.

The city's defenders closed the gates and guarded its walls. It is said they blocked the Bosphorus river that ran through the city with gigantic chains. But the Rus moved their ships past this blockage on rollers.

The Rus attacked the edge of the city, setting fire to its churches and palaces. They slaughtered many people. Bodies were thrown into the water.

Finally, to avoid further bloodshed, the city elders offered Oleg a deal, allowing his people riches, free accommodation and tax-free trade in their markets. Oleg raised his shield above the city gates to claim victory.

VARANGIAN GUARD

During the 10th-12th centuries, Viking warriors took on the role of an elite bodyguard for the Byzantine emperor. These fighters were named the Varangian Guard.

The Varangian warriors were first employed by Byzantine Emperor Basil II to help put down local revolts and fight foreign armies. He called them "Varangian", which means "men of the pledge".

This Varangian warrior wears chain mail, plus splint-armour metal defences for his arms and legs.

Long, two-handed axe with a crescent-shaped blade. The Varangians were referred to as the "axe-bearing barbarians".

This picture from an 11th-century Greek history book shows the Varangian guard on duty.

The 1500-year-old former church of Hagia Sophia in Istanbul stills stands but is now a mosque. There are Viking runes etched on a bannister inside, thought to have been made by the Varangian guard.

GODS AND GODDESSES

The Vikings believed that the universe was ruled by many gods and goddesses. The stories of these gods were told in ancient legends and sagas.

Odin was the oldest and most powerful of the gods. He rode an eight-legged horse called Sleipnir and ruled over a majestic banqueting hall called Valhalla. The Vikings believed that warriors who died in battle would travel to Valhalla to feast.

Loki was the son of giants, and foster brother of Thor. He enjoyed playing tricks on the other gods and causing trouble.

Thor was the most important god for Viking warriors. He wielded a mighty hammer that caused the rumble of thunder. He also drove a chariot driven by two goats.

Frey was the god of fertility. He owned a magical ship that could carry all the gods, yet could be shrunk to pocket size.

In Viking legends, Valkyries were female warriors who flew over the battlefields gathering souls of the dead before carrying them to Valhalla.

VIKING UNIVERSE

The Vikings called Earth Midgard (Middle Earth) and believed it was joined to eight other worlds populated by gods, dwarves, giants and elves. At the centre of the Viking universe was Yggdrasil, a huge ash tree that held the different worlds together.

Asgard was the home of the Aesir gods, led by Odin. Asgard was joined to Midgard by Bifrost, a rainbow bridge. Only the gods could cross it.

Vanaheim was home to the lesser Vanir gods. They were the gods of farmers and fishermen, and they had the power to see into the future.

Svartalfheim was lived in by the underground-dwelling dark elves. They made unbreakable chains softer than ribbon.

The land of Nidavellir was home to the dwarves. They were the great blacksmiths who forged Thor's hammer.

The branches of Yggdrasil were home to creatures, such as a wise eagle and a stag.

Valhalla, the majestic hall ruled over by the god Odin.

Alfheim was home to the light elves whose magical powers inspired people to create art and music.

Midgard, the land of men, was created by Odin and his brothers Vili and Ve. It was encircled by a giant serpent.

Jotunheim was the land of rock-giants who menaced both gods and men.

Niflheim was the icy underworld of the dead, where the frost-giants lived.

Muspell was the flaming world of fire, ruled by the fire giant, Surt.

FAMOUS VIKINGS

Though the Vikings left few written records, the names of some Vikings are still famous, centuries later. Eric Bloodaxe was known for his ruthlessness and for ruling his subjects with an iron fist. Harald Hardrada was a strong leader with a reputation for crushing his enemies.

Eric Bloodaxe slaughtered four of his brothers to take the Norwegian throne. Eric later fled to England where he became King of Northumbria with his capital city at York.

In AD 947 Eadred, King of England, launched an attack on Eric and persuaded the people to reject his rule. However, Eric seized the throne again in AD 952. His rule did not last long, however, as he was killed at the Battle of Stainmore in AD 954.

Eric Bloodaxe
AD 885-954

In AD 1030, at the age of 15, Harald Hardrada fought and killed his brother, the Norwegian king. He then became a military commander in Kiev and later a Varangian guard. He made a fortune through raiding.

In AD 1047 Harald became King of Norway but also had his eye on the Danish throne. He spent 20 years fighting the King of Denmark. In 1066 Harald invaded England. He was defeated and killed at the Battle of Stamford Bridge by the English king. Harald is often seen as the last great Viking leader.

Harald Hardrada
AD 1015-1066

CHRISTIANITY

During the 11th century, Christianity spread to Scandinavia. Viking leaders realised that they could gain more influence with neighbouring countries if they stopped worshipping their old gods and adopted Christianity. The rise of Christianity signalled the end of the great age of the Vikings.

Christianity was known to Viking traders. They had seen cathedrals on their travels and some traders wore crosses to help them trade in Christian markets. Vikings who settled in England and Ireland gradually adopted Christian beliefs.

King Harald Bluetooth of Denmark wanted proof of the Christian god's power. It is said that a priest named Poppo performed a miracle in front of him by holding a red-hot iron in his bare hands without being burned. King Harald converted around AD 965, as shown in this 11th-century gold plate.

The Norwegian king Olaf II Haraldsson (right) was keen to convert his people to Christianity. After his death he was made patron saint of Norway.

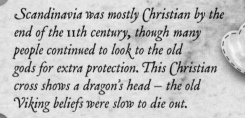

Scandinavia was mostly Christian by the end of the 11th century, though many people continued to look to the old gods for extra protection. This Christian cross shows a dragon's head – the old Viking beliefs were slow to die out.

As Christians, the Vikings built churches. This 12th-century church in Borgund, Norway, was made out of wooden planks.

VIKING BURIAL

The Vikings believed that the dead would journey to the afterlife. Important Vikings were buried in ships that were meant to carry them to the next world. They were also buried with tools, personal possessions and even animals that they might need in their next life.

Archaeologists have discovered Viking treasures, tools and animal remains inside burial ship graves. Some Vikings were buried with a servant to make the journey with them.

The Vikings set fire to burial ships. They thought the dead would then rise with the smoke to Odin's hall, Valhalla. The remains of the ship were buried in mounds of earth, like these in Gamla Uppsala, Sweden.

This wagon was discovered in a Viking burial ship in Oseberg, Norway.

In 1903, archaeologists discovered a huge burial ship at Oseberg. Made from trees felled in AD 834, it measured 21m long and 5m wide. Inside they found a host of treasure along with the skeletons of two Viking noblewomen.

Poorer Vikings were often cremated and buried with just a knife or a brooch. Their final resting place may have been marked with stones in the shape of a ship, as in this field of 700 graves in Lindholm, Denmark.

Every January, the people of Shetland off the north coast of Scotland hold a Viking celebration. Locals dressed as Viking warriors carry flaming torches through the streets and hurl them aboard a replica longship to set it alight. This celebration, known as Up Helly Aa, first started in 1870.

The publishers would like to thank the following sources for their kind permission to reproduce the pictures in this book.

p1 © Carlton Books, p2 SuperStock/Nordic Photos (rune stone), p2 The Art Archive/Gianni Dagli Orti (top left and p3 centre), p3 Getty Images/Gallo Images (top right), p4 Getty Images/Werner Forman (bottom left), p5 Corbis/Werner Forman (centre right), p5 Getty Images/Dorling Kindersley (bottom right), p6 © Carlton Books (helmet & chain-mail), p6 Alamy/YAY Media AS (shield), p6 Getty Images/Dorling Kindersley (Axe), p6 AKG-Images/Interfoto/Hermann Historica GmbH (sword), pg6 The Bridgeman Art Library/Ancient Art and Architecture Collection Ltd. (boot), p7 The Bridgeman Art Library/ © National Museums of Scotland (top), p7. Getty Images/ Dorling Kindersley (bottom), p8 The Bridgeman Art Library/Werner Forman (necklace), p8. The Art Archive/Prehistoric Museum Moesgard Højbjerg Denmark/Gianni Dagli Orti (comb), p8 Getty Images/ Werner Forman (brooch), p8 AKG-Images/Interfoto/Hermann Historica GmbH (ring), p9 Shutterstock, p11 Getty Images/Universal Images Group (bottom), p11 The Bridgeman Art Library/National Museum of Ireland, Dublin, Ireland/Photo © Boltin Picture Library (top), p11 The Bridgeman Art Library/Ancient Art and Architecture Collection Ltd. (bottom right), p12 Getty Images/Gallo Images (cattle), p12 Thinkstock (top right), p12 Alamy/Ladi Kirn (bottom right), p14 Corbis/Ted Spiegel, p16 The Bridgeman Art Library/Viking Ship Museum, Oslo, Norway (top), p16 The Bridgeman Art Library/ Nationalmuseet, Copenhagen, Denmark (bottom), p17 Getty Images/ Werner Forman (top left, centre left & right), p17 Corbis/Ted Spiegel (top right), p17 The Bridgeman Art Library/Kunstindustrimuseet, Oslo, Norway, p18 The Bridgeman Art Library/© Look and Learn (bottom left), p18 Alamy/Rolf Richardson (bottom right), p20 Getty Images/ Lonely Planet Images (left), p20 SuperStock/Nordic Photos (right), p20 Scala Archives/De Agostini Picture Library (bottom left), p21 Private Collection (top), p21 Corbis/Werner Forman (bottom left), p21 Bridgeman Art Library/British Library, London, UK (right), p21 Bridgeman Art Library/Private Collection (bottom right), p22 & p23 Private Collection, p24 Mary Evans/M.C.Esteban/Iberfoto (left), p24 Alamy/Gezmen (right), p25 Bridgeman Art Library/Ancient Art and Architecture Collection Ltd., p25 Getty Images/Werner Forman (top right), p25 Getty Images/De Agostini (bottom left), p25 Getty Images (bottom right), p29 AKG-Images/Interfoto (centre left), p29 Alamy/ Zoonar GmbH (bottom right), p29 The Bridgeman Art Library/De Agostini Picture Library/A. Dagli Orti (top right), p29 Bridgeman Art Library/National Museum of Iceland, Reykjavik, Iceland (bottom left), p30 Bridgeman Art Library/Private Collection (top left), p30 Cultural Museum Oslo (right), p30 Alamy/picturesbyrob (centre left), p30 Getty Images/Werner Forman (bottom), p31 Corbis/Ted Spiegel (top), p31 Thinkstock (centre), p31 Getty Images/Britain on View

Every effort has been made to acknowledge correctly and contact the source and/or copyright holder of each picture and Carlton Books Limited apologises for any unintentional errors or omissions, which will be corrected in future editions of this book.

CARLTON KiDS

This is a Carlton book.
Text, design and illustration © Carlton Books Limited 2014

Published in 2014 by Carlton Books Limited,
an imprint of the Carlton Publishing Group,
20 Mortimer Street, London W1T 3JW.

A catalogue record is available for this book from the British Library.

Printed and bound in Heshan, China
ISBN: 978-1-78312-084-0

Illustrations: Peter Liddiard

Executive Editor: Selina Wood
Managing Art Editor: Jake Da'Costa
Designer: Zoë Dissell
Consultant: John Malam
Production: Ena Matagic